The Big Strawberry Book of
Dinosaurs and Other Prehistoric Animals

Printed in the United States of America
Library of Congress Catalog Card Number: 77-93626
ISBN: Trade 0-88470-055-0. Library 0-88470-056-9. Paperback 0-88470-057-7

The Big Strawberry Book of

DINOSAURS

and Other Prehistoric Animals

Written by Sidney Horenstein • Illustrated by Matthew Kalmenoff

Strawberry Books distributed by Larousse & Co., Inc. New York

Contents

Introduction

Eusthenopteron

Dinosaurs were animals that lived many millions of years ago. There were many different kinds of dinosaurs, some as small as a chicken, some almost as big as a whale. Now there are no dinosaurs left on earth. How do we know about dinosaurs?

We know about them because people have found dinosaur bones in rocks. We call these ancient bones fossils.

The men and women who study fossils are called paleontologists (pal-ee-on-TOLL-o-jists). After a paleontologist collects a fossil he or she will give it an identifying number and write down all the information about its location in a notebook.

A fossil is any remains or impression, such as a bone or footprint of an animal or plant, that is usually more than ten thousand years old.

Once the fossil is at home or in a laboratory the paleontologist may want to remove additional rock around the fossil so that it can be seen more clearly. The fossil may also require special treatment to help preserve it for the future.

Most likely the fossil has already been named. Once in a while a paleontologist will find an animal or plant that has never been named before. The paleontologist must then give it a new name.

All plants and animals on this earth are given scientific names in Latin or Greek, two ancient languages. For example, *Tyrannosaurus,* from the Latin, which means ''tyrant lizard'' in English, will be spelled *Tyrannosaurus* whether the scientist is American, English, Swedish, Russian, or French.

Most of the time the name of the animal or plant tells us something about it. Occasionally an animal or plant may be named after a person or place. The name of the person or place is then translated into Latin so that people all over the world will use the same word to describe it. Sometimes the name may make no sense at all because some scientists in the past never said what the name meant.

In the Beginning

Dinosaurs lived many millions of years ago, long before there were people or any of the animals that we know today.

It is very difficult to imagine millions of years. Try to think of time as a very tall building, 100 floors high. To get to the top it would take us 50 million years between each floor! Not until we get to the 36th floor (about 3,200,000,000 years ago) would we find the first evidence of life.

At the 88th floor (in what scientists call the Paleozoic era) the first animals, those without backbones, such as the extinct trilobite, primitive snails, lamp shells—which look like today's clams—and colonies of corals appear. These are followed by primitive fish, the first vertebrates, 460 million years ago. The vertebrates appear on the 91st floor of our building.

As we approach the 92nd floor, about 450 million years ago, life is able to invade the land in the form of plants and insects.

About 225 million years ago (between the 95th and 96th floors) we meet the first mammals. Between the 96th and 97th floors the first flowering plants appear.

As we get close to the last stories of our building mammals appear in all their varieties. Men and women, the newcomers, appear as we approach the 100th floor.

We have been comparing time to a 100-story building. When geologists discuss the history of life, they divide time into four great eras: the Precambrian (1st to 88th floors), the Paleozoic (88th to 95th floors), the Mesozoic (95th to 98½ floors) and the Cenozoic (98½ to 100th floors). They then divide the eras into smaller units called "periods" and the periods into smaller units called "epochs."

Eusthenopteron

From Fish to Amphibian

The earliest-known fossil fish was found in rocks formed during Early Ordovician time in what is now known as the Soviet Union.

Some of the early fish from Early Devonian time lived in shallow freshwater streams and lakes. Sometimes the water dried up. Some fish learned to travel across land on their stubby fins to find water. They had lungs so they could breathe air.

Eusthenopteron (you-sthen-OP-ter-on, ''strong fin'') in the picture is a good example of a fish that had strong ''lobe'' fins (with fleshy bases that were like the beginnings of feet) and lungs. It was able to drag itself slowly over the ground in search of water.

Gradually, after many thousands of years, these fish evolved into amphibians. They grew short arms and legs instead of fins, skin that wouldn't dry out in air, and strong skeletons to support their bodies on land. An amphibian is an animal that lays jellylike eggs in or near water. The young usually live in water and breathe through gills. The adults usually live on land and breathe through lungs.

Ichthyostega (ick-thee-o-STEE-guh, ''hidden fish'') in the picture is an example of this kind of new amphibian. It is the ancestor of the salamanders, toads, and frogs we know today.

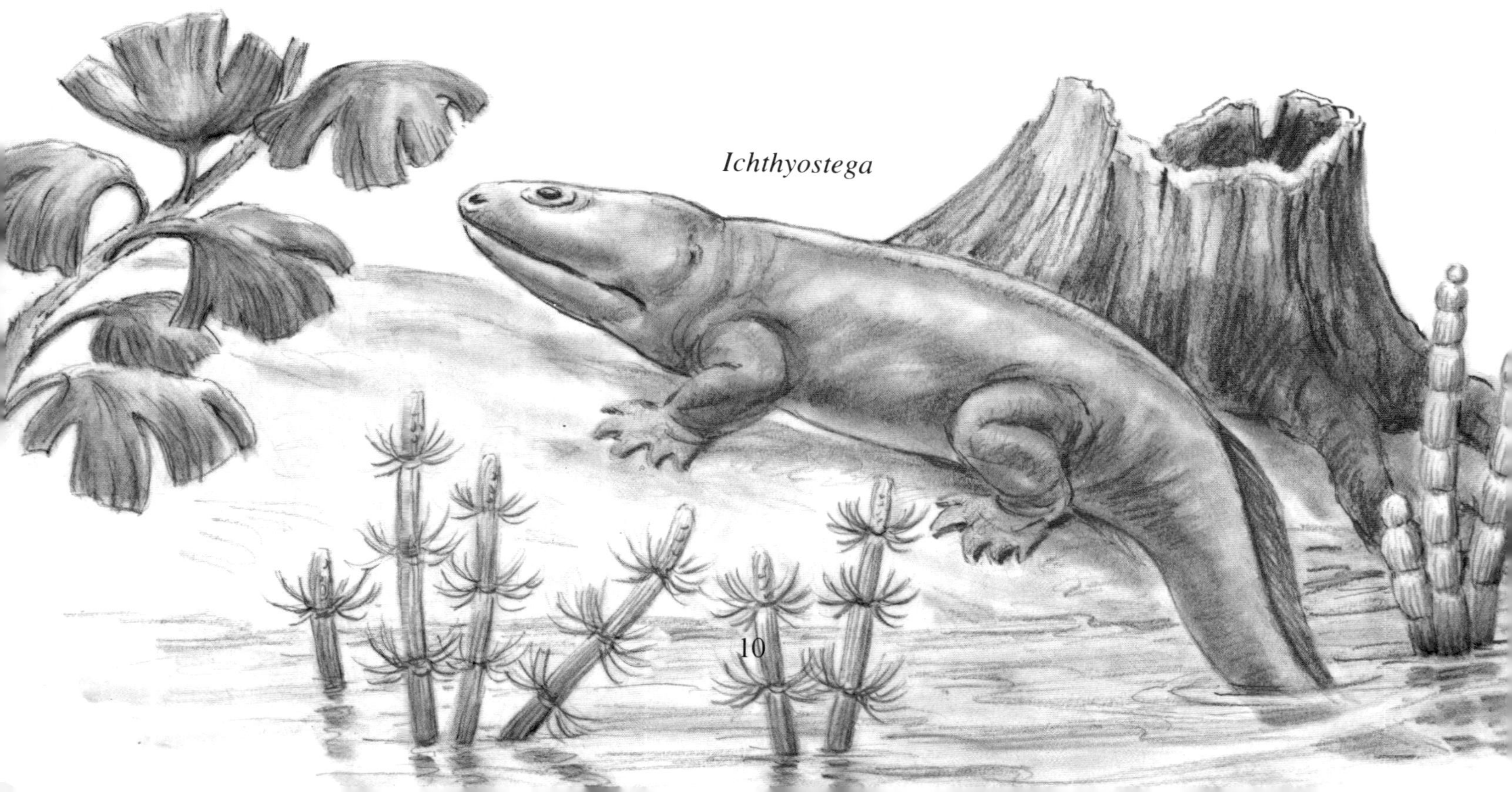

Ichthyostega

Eryops

In the center of the illustration is *Eryops* (EAR-ee-ops, "raised eye"), the best-known fossil amphibian. It lived during the early part of the Permian period, about 270 million years ago. The fossil remains of *Eryops* are found in Texas.

Eryops looks like an overgrown salamander with a long sloping face. It was about six feet (less than two meters) long and weighed perhaps as much as 150 pounds (about 70 kilograms). Its squat body hugged the ground and its thick, short, and strong limbs were set far apart. Not only did its leathery skin give it protection from its meat-eating neighbors but it allowed *Eryops* to spend some time out of water without drying up.

Fossil remains of amphibians very much like *Eryops* have been found in places as far apart as Texas (U.S.A.) and Czechoslovakia (Europe). These finds make scientists believe that at one time the continents were joined together, though now they have drifted away from one another and are separated by oceans.

Eryops

Seymouria

From Water to Land

All amphibians must live close to the water. Their soft, jellylike eggs are laid in or near the water. When the eggs hatch the young continue to live in or near the water. Even when they become adults few amphibians stray far from the water. Frogs, toads, and salamanders are modern-day amphibians.

This characteristic of being completely dependent on water is what chiefly distinguishes amphibians from reptiles. Reptiles evolved from amphibians. That is, after many centuries of gradual change a creature became so different from the amphibians that it was given another name.

What made the big difference between reptiles and amphibians?

It was the egg, the amniote egg. This kind of egg did not have to be laid in water. It had a hard shell. It could be laid on land, so the new creature was able to move further inland, away from the water. All birds and most reptiles lay amniote eggs.

The word "amniote" comes from the name of one of the skinlike "sacs" that holds the embryo as it develops inside the shell.

The egg is really a marvelous thing to know about. The outer covering, the shell, helps protect the developing embryo from bumps and jolts. It is the baby chicken's suit of armor. Strong as it is, the shell is porous. That means it allows air to go in and out so that the embryo can breathe.

The yellow yolk inside the shell is the embryo's food supply. The embryo floats in a watery substance within the egg (the "white" of the egg) that is like a small lake or ocean inside a shell. Once the eggshell is broken, the baby bird or reptile can soon move around freely, seeking its own food. (Baby frogs, called tadpoles, and other amphibians must live in the water until they become adult.)

Although you can tell a present-day reptile from an amphibian by its skeleton as well as by its soft parts, this distinction is not possible with some

Diadectes

of the earliest reptiles, whose soft parts have disappeared.

It is very difficult to know if a "reptile" fossil was in fact a reptile. Many creatures that are thought to be reptiles have skeletons that look like those of early amphibians. It is also difficult to tell, from its fossilized remains, if an animal laid an amniote egg or laid its egg in the water.

The remains of *Seymouria* (see-MORE-ee-ya), named after Seymour, Texas, where it was found, has been classified as a reptile *and* as an amphibian because its skeleton looks a little like both that of a reptile and an amphibian. Today, most specialists agree that *Seymouria* is an advanced amphibian rather than an early reptile. *Seymouria* was a meat-eater about the size of a collie dog.

As you can see, scientists who study old bones can never be very sure of anything, because the animals they study have all disappeared from the earth, and they must use intelligent guesswork.

Diadectes (dye-a-DEK-tees, "across biter") was a heavy, squat animal that lived during the Early Permian period. It had strong five-toed feet that supported its six-foot (less than two meters) body. *Diadectes* was probably a plant-eater. It had peglike front teeth it used for biting off plants and back teeth that could grind and crush. *Diadectes,* like *Seymouria,* was a reptile that had features of both reptiles and amphibians.

Eventually enough information will be found as new skeletons are discovered in the rocks. Scientists will be able to tell exactly how *Seymouria* and *Diadectes* fit into the picture of evolving amphibians and reptiles.

On the next page is a chart showing the main features of reptile evolution. The animals at the top are today's surviving reptiles, leftovers after millions of years of history.

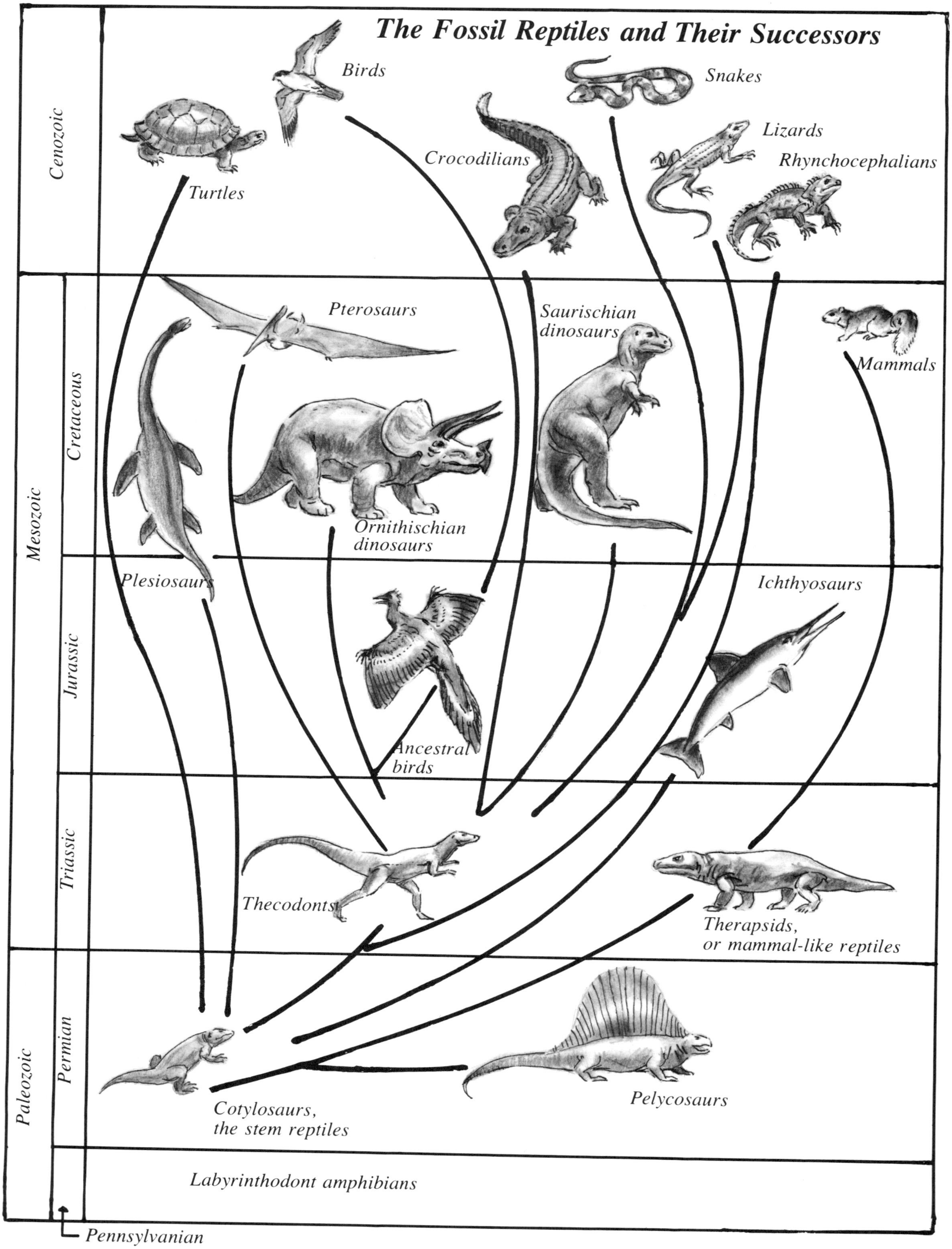
The Fossil Reptiles and Their Successors
Cenozoic
Mesozoic
Paleozoic
Cretaceous
Jurassic
Triassic
Permian
Pennsylvanian
Birds
Snakes
Lizards
Rhynchocephalians
Crocodilians
Turtles
Pterosaurs
Saurischian dinosaurs
Mammals
Ornithischian dinosaurs
Plesiosaurs
Ichthyosaurs
Ancestral birds
Thecodonts
Therapsids, or mammal-like reptiles
Cotylosaurs, the stem reptiles
Pelycosaurs
Labyrinthodont amphibians

The Cotylosaurs

The first reptiles are known as cotylosaurs (ko--TIE-lo-sawrs, ''cup lizards,'' because of the cup-shaped depressions on the vertebrae bones in some animals of the group). They are also called the stem reptiles because all other reptiles evolved from them, as branches and twigs come out from the main stem of a plant. Many of them looked like their heavy-limbed amphibian ancestors, such as *Seymouria* described on page 12.

The cotylosaurs are found in many parts of the world. They lived from the beginning of Pennsylvanian time to the end of the Triassic period. *Hylonomus* (hi-lo-NO-mus, ''wood name''), one of the earliest reptiles, is described on pages 16 and 17.

Captorhinus (kap-toe-RINE-us, ''eat quickly snout'') belongs to a group of cotylosaurs that gave rise to most of the future reptiles and probably to mammals, including human beings. You can tell that it was a meat-eater by the many sharp, pointed teeth in its jaws. Its food consisted of large insects, amphibians, and reptiles. The reptiles it ate had to be smaller than *Captorhinus,* which was two feet (about 58 centimeters) long. *Captorhinus* lived during Early Permian time in Texas and New Mexico.

Not all of the cotylosaurs were small. *Limnoscelis* (lim-NOSS-el-is, ''marsh leg'') shared the same environment as *Captorhinus*. It grew to be five feet (about one and one half meters) long. *Limnoscelis* was a semi-aquatic animal, a clumsy creature on land, more at ease in the water. Its habits were probably like the crocodiles', as were so many of the early reptiles. It had rows of sharp teeth in its jaws, with which it ate the amphibians that abounded in its watery home.

The first major plant-eating group of reptiles appeared during the middle of Permian time. Some of them were small, less than a foot long, but others grew to be at least 10 feet (about three meters) long.

They did not live very long: They became extinct by the time the Permian period was over. These vegetarians have been found in Europe and Africa.

Bradysaurus (bray-dee-SAWR-us, ''slow lizard''), from South Africa, is typical of this group. About eight or nine feet (more than two and one half meters) long, it was heavy, short-tailed, and had a big belly. All plant-eaters tend to have large bodies. Plants have to remain in their stomachs for a long time because plants are hard to digest. *Bradysaurus* also had the peglike teeth common to most plant-eaters. These teeth were used to crush and grind tough plant fibers.

Bradysaurus probably weighed more than a ton (about 900 kilograms). It lived in swamps where there was plenty of vegetation. Some of its relatives have been preserved right side up with their legs beneath their bodies. How could this happen? Perhaps the creature was wading though the swamp, munching on the vegetation. It came to a place where it got stuck in the mud, sank into it, and was buried.

All of the cotylosaur families, except one, died out during the Permian period. One family lasted to nearly the end of the Triassic. *Hypsognathus* (hip-so-NAY-thus, ''high jaw'') is one of these. It reminds scientists a little of the horned toads that are found in the deserts of the southwestern United States. Like the horned toads, *Hypsognathus* had spikes on the sides and back of its flattish skull. Horned toads are not toads but lizards, and *Hypsognathus* is not a lizard but a cotylosaur. Some of these one-foot-long reptiles are found in Late Triassic rocks across the Hudson River from New York City.

Cotylosaurs—Hylonomus

In Nova Scotia, Canada, near the town of Joggins, there are miles of high cliffs along the shoreline of the Bay of Fundy. The rocks these cliffs are made of were formed during the Pennsylvanian period about 300 million years ago.

The fossil remains of *Hylonomus,* one of the earliest known reptiles, are found in these cliffs.

You can get a good idea of the way *Hylonomus* looked and acted by studying the smaller lizards that are in the iguana family. Use the painting on this page to help you pick them out. Just like most modern iguanas, *Hylonomus* probably fed on insects and other invertebrate animals that lived in and on the soil. *Hylonomus* could grow to be about the size of a man's shoe, about 12 inches (almost 30 centimeters) long.

If you go to Nova Scotia to look for the fossil bones of *Hylonomus,* you will have to search in a very unusual place. Fossil bones are found in the hollow stumps of fossil trees called *Lycopods* (LIE-co-pods). The ancient plants called *Lycopods* are still living today. They are known as club moss, although the name means ''wolf's foot.''

Club moss is found mostly in tropical climates. The plants are small and grow close to the ground. During Pennsylvanian time they flourished as large trees. Some grew to be 100 feet (a little more than 30 meters) tall and had a diameter of three or four feet (around one meter). The trees grew on low, swampy land as well as on slightly higher, drier ground.

During the early part of the Pennsylvanian period there were many earth movements in this part of North America. When the land moved down, it became flooded and covered over with a thick blanket of mud up to 20 feet (about six meters) in thickness. When the land rose it dried out. The climate was warm. Great forests of *Lycopods* and other types of extinct trees grew here. *Hylonomus* lived on the higher, drier ground. Every time the land was flooded the animal would seek shelter elsewhere and wait for the flood waters to recede or dry up.

A thick layer of mud buried the base of trees in the flooded areas and killed many of them. When they died, the inside wood of the trees rotted away and the trees came crashing down, breaking off at the new surface of the ground. The buried hollow stumps became big holes in the ground.

When *Hylonomus* and other reptiles and amphibians fell into these pits they usually could not get out. We know that they were alive when they fell in and not washed in by the flood after they died because the pits contain a large amount of coprolites—fossil excrement.

The pits filled in later during the next flood and the animals were buried and fossilized. There are about 50 buried forests exposed along the cliffs, near Joggins, in Nova Scotia. So far only 30 tree stumps have been found with fossils, but together they contain hundreds of specimens of amphibians and reptiles.

Mammal-like Reptiles

Near the end of the Pennsylvanian period a new group of reptiles appeared. They are called the pelycosaurs (pel-i-CO-sawrs, ''basin lizards''). They evolved rapidly into a large number of different kinds of early reptiles. Some of them were plant-eaters and the others were meat-eaters. By the time the next period, the Permian, was ending the pelycosaurs were extinct. Their descendants were the therapsids.

The word ''therapsid'' (thair-AP-sid) means ''beast opening.'' The name was given to this reptile because it has an opening in its skull similar to the holes in the skulls of mammals. The therapsids evolved from meat-eating pelycosaurs and, just like them, evolved into many different kinds of reptiles. Some of them became plant-eaters, too. At some time during the beginning of the Jurassic period, the therapsids disappeared, but it was from this group that mammals, including human beings, evolved.

The therapsids are also called mammal-like reptiles even though they didn't look particularly like mammals. They are given this name because they have many features in their skeletons that are similar to mammals.

As well as the hole in the skull, they had, like mammals, a variety of teeth. Some of their teeth were used for chewing and others were used for stabbing and slicing. This specialization of teeth is more a mammal characteristic than reptilian. Reptiles usually have teeth that are all pretty much the same; they tend to swallow their food whole. Mammals, on the other hand, usually slice and chew their food and swallow small pieces.

Touch the roof of your mouth with your tongue. This part of your mouth is called the palate. It separates your nasal passages from your mouth. This is one of the features of mammal-like reptiles. They also had a palate that separated the breathing passages from the eating and swallowing passages. This enabled them to breathe properly while eating, which most reptiles cannot do.

The therapsids are sometimes called the advanced mammal-like reptiles and the pelycosaurs the primitive mammal-like reptiles. *Dimetrodon* (die-MEET-ro-don ''two-measure teeth,'' because their teeth were of two different sizes), described on pages 20–21, belongs to the group of pelycosaurs that gave rise to the therapsids.

The mammal-like reptiles were the dominant group of land animals of their time. They evolved into a great variety of animals, probably as great as the variety of dinosaurs that was to replace them as the lords of the land from the end of the Triassic period to the end of the Cretaceous. Some of the last therapsids lived side by side with some of the early dinosaurs.

Mammal

Mammal-like Reptile

Reptile

Cynognathus (sine-o-NAY-thus, "dog jaw") is usually thought of as the typical therapsid that looks most like a mammal. It grew to the size of a large German shepherd. Some people with good imaginations think it looked a little like a dog. As you can see from the illustration, *Cynognathus* must have been a menace to many other animals. It had powerful jaws and a pair of tusks that were useful for stabbing. In front of the tusks were teeth for nipping, and in back of them were teeth for chewing and cutting. It is also possible that *Cynognathus* ate vegetables as well as meat. It lived in South Africa during Early and Middle Triassic times and became extinct before the first mammals appeared in the Late Triassic. We believe that one of its relatives evolved into a mammal, but we don't know which one. Eventually the fossil hunters may find the "missing link."

Moschops (MOSS-kops, "calf face") was another vegetarian. It lived in South Africa during the Permian period. It grew to be about eight feet (almost two and one half meters) long, with shoulders much higher than its rear end. Its great back sloped downward from neck to tail. Its back and broad feet and heavy limbs must have made *Moschops* a very clumsy-looking animal as it roamed the landscape munching on vegetation with its peglike teeth.

Moschops

Cynognathus

Lystrosaurus (lys-trow-SAWR-us) lived during the early Triassic period. It was about three or four feet (about one meter) long and had a thick body. It stood on short, strong legs, and its feet flared out a little. Its head was flattened; its nostrils were high up in front of its eyes. Two large tusks, the only teeth it had, stuck out of its mouth. Its jaws looked like the smooth beaks that turtles have. *Lystrosaurus* lived in swamps, rivers, and lakes, behaving somewhat like a small hippopotamus, eating vegetation. The front of its mouth was useful for pulling and cutting plants. Next time you go to the zoo, see where the hippopotamus' nostrils are located: high up in front of its eyes so it can breathe while eating underwater plants.

Lystrosaurus has been found in India, China, Africa, and Antarctica. It seems likely that all these places may have been joined together when *Lystrosaurus* lived, since it could not swim the ocean.

Lystrosaurus

Mammal-like Reptiles— Dimetrodon

The most terrifying reptile that lived in the Permian period was *Dimetrodon*. As you can see in the illustration, it had a large head; its teeth looked like daggers and were used like them. *Eryops* (see page 11) would have made a nice meal for *Dimetrodon,* but *Eryops* probably got away easily because it could swim.

Dimetrodon couldn't hide very well. It didn't have to. It was the biggest animal in the neighborhood.

The most unusual part of *Dimetrodon* was its sail. The paleontologist who first studied *Dimetrodon* thought of several reasons for the purpose of the sail. He jokingly suggested that it was used to go sailing on the shallow Permian lakes.

Since then scientists who have studied *Dimetrodon* have come up with a more reasonable explanation for the purpose of the sail: It was a natural "air conditioner" that helped keep the animal's body temperature comfortable.

All reptiles living today are cold-blooded, and so were most fossil reptiles. Reptiles have no way to keep their body temperature constant the way mammals do. On cold days they drag themselves into the sun so they can warm up and become active. When they get too hot, they crawl into the shade to cool off.

The bones that supported *Dimetrodon*'s sails

were not jointed. They could not be folded down but remained in a straight-up position. A thin layer of skin covered the bones, giving it a sail-like appearance. Blood moving through the thin skin of the sail would become cooler on a hot day as the air swept over the sail.

But the sail could also keep *Dimetrodon* warm on days that got too cold. On a cool day, the sun's rays beat down on the sail, heated it up and by doing so heated the blood also. Some scientists believe *Dimetrodon* could control the amount of heating and cooling because it could control the amount of blood that pulsed through the sail.

This is a scene during Early Permian time in Texas. The large carnivorous *Dimetrodon* is looking over its territory. *Edaphosaurus* (ee-DAF-o-sawr-us, ''base lizard''), with smaller, curved fins, has crossbars on its spines. Unlike *Dimetrodon, Edaphosaurus* was a vegetarian. *Ophiacodon* (o-fee-AK-o-don, ''snake tooth''), a pelycosaur and close relative, is prowling the shoreline for fish and shellfish. *Eryops* and *Cacops* (cay-KOPS,''bad eye''), amphibians, are keeping a watchful eye out for *Dimetrodon*. *Captorhinus,* the small carnivorous cotylosaur, is watching out for *Dimetrodon* and waiting for *Eryops* and *Cacops* to pass its way.

Lizards, Snakes, Turtles, and Their Relatives

Lizards and snakes are the most numerous modern reptiles. There are about 3,000 species of lizards and about 2,700 species of snakes.

One of the first lizards was *Icarosaurus* (IK-ar-o-sawr-us, "Icarus lizard") named after Icarus, a character in a Greek myth who made himself wings of wax and feathers that melted when he flew too close to the sun. As you can see, the lizard *Icarosaurus* had wings. It could not use them to fly. It climbed trees that grew around a giant lake in New Jersey during the Late Triassic period and would glide from branch to branch. A similar creature has been found in Great Britain.

Some animals living today can do the same thing, such as the gliding lizard *Draco* (DRAY-co, "dragon"). There are even "flying" snakes and "flying" squirrels that glide with the help of flaps of skin on their bodies. *Icarosaurus* was about the size of the squirrel that you have probably seen in parks. The ribs of *Icarosaurus* were very long; its skin was stretched over them to form the wings. When it had no use for its wings it could fold them up along the side of its body and slink around on its feet.

Another strange animal, a lizardlike reptile from Europe, is called *Tanystropheus* (tan-ee-STROFE-ee-us, which means "long vertebrae"). As you can see, it had a very long neck, and, in fact, it had little else. One scientist jokingly suggested that it cleaned out drain pipes. Although many specimens are two or three feet (less than one meter) long, there are reports that suggest that they may have grown to more than 20 feet (over six meters) in length. They were probably good at catching insects and maybe even fish, because they could move their heads quickly. They didn't have many bones for such a long neck; the bones were just longer, like those of a giraffe. *Tanystropheus* lived during the middle part of the Triassic period.

Some lizards went to sea and grew to be 50 or more feet (over 15 meters) long. One group is known as the mosasaurs (MOZE-a-sawrs, "Meuse River Lizards"). (See pages 24–25.)

The animals discussed above are examples of the great variety of forms that lizards gradually took after they first appeared. By Jurassic times they already resembled some lizards that we see today. Unlike other reptiles, such as the dinosaurs, the lizards and snakes survived the great Cretaceous extinction and went on to flourish and increase their species.

Boa

Snakes first appeared in Early Cretaceous time. Some scientists think that the ancestors of the snakes were lizards that lived in burrows below the ground. There they gradually lost their legs and grew more ribs and vertebrae (backbones). After the snakes evolved in this way they adapted to life above the ground. Perhaps food was plentiful and there were few enemies. These early snakes were probably like boa constrictors and pythons. Snakes can be recognized easily in fossils. Most of these early remains consist of vertebrae and ribs. There are no known poisonous snakes during the early history of snakes. Poison, which is an important characteristic of some snakes, developed later, perhaps 40 million years ago.

This is an illustration of a modern boa: It may grow as long as 30 feet (more than nine meters), and it probably looks like the ancient snakes. Paleontologists use living animals as models to give form to ancient creatures. When there are no living relatives, it is very difficult to imagine how muscles and skin fitted over strange old bones.

If turtles did not exist today and you were the first paleontologist to find a turtle shell, how would you reconstruct this animal? Would it look like a turtle or some other creature? These are questions that paleontologists like to ask their students. They get many unusual and interesting answers.

The first known turtles were found in Middle Triassic rocks in Germany. *Proganochelys* (pro-GAN-o-kellys, ''early turtle'') already looked like a modern turtle with its protective shell. It was about two feet (about 60 centimeters) long. Like the turtles that live today, it had no teeth along the sides of its jaw. It is the only known turtle with some teeth on its palate (the roof of the mouth). Its skull was about five or six inches (about 12 or 14 centimeters) long, and its head was covered with bony plates. Unlike modern turtles, it could not draw its limbs and head into its shell, but projections from the shell and bony coverings on its limbs and head gave *Proganochelys* some protection.

Turtles live in rivers, marshes, dry land, forests, and deserts. The seagoing turtles come to land to lay their eggs. Some are very small and others gigantic. Some eat only meat; others, only vegetables; and others, anything.

One group of turtles became extinct at the end of the last ice age, only about 10,000 years ago.

The largest known turtle is called *Archelon* (AR-kee-lon, ''ruler turtle''). It lived in the sea that covered part of Kansas during the Late Cretaceous period, about 80,000,000 years ago. It grew to be more than 12 feet (almost four meters) long. Its huge flippers tell us that it must have been an excellent swimmer. Its shell was not as heavy as some, since it was one of the turtles that lost most of its protective armor. Some scientists estimate that it weighed about three tons (about 2,700 kilograms)—approximately the weight of two medium-sized cars. It must have been some sight to see huge *Archelon* coming ashore to lay eggs.

Proganochelys

Mosasaurs
Pteranodon
Archelon
Tylosaurus

The lizards that went back to the sea grew to great lengths. They had a variety of shapes, but their common features were a large head that was long and sort of pointed, a medium-sized neck, and a long body and tail. They swam the way we think a sea serpent would. The tail and body moved from side to side. The arms and legs gradually evolved into flippers that were used to steer the animal and that enabled it to make sharp turns.

One 20-foot-long (over six meters) mosasaur lived in a sea that covered Kansas during Late Cretaceous time. Its name is *Tylosaurus* (TILE-o-sawr-us, ''knot lizard''), and judging from the great number of knifelike teeth in its mouth, it was truly a sea monster. It ate fish. In fact, mosasaurs evolved at the same time that bony fish were evolving rapidly into a number of different kinds. Some scientists believe that *Tylosaurus* was able to eat fish that weighed as much as 800 pounds (about 365 kilograms). It certainly could swallow them, since its lower jaw had a special hinge that allowed it to open its mouth very wide.

Fish were not *Tylosaurus*' only food. Fossils of giant shellfish that are now extinct have been found with the teeth marks of *Tylosaurus* on them. It must have grabbed them in its teeth, which it used to crush the shell and squeeze out the soft animal in the shell. It would not be surprising if it even had tried its luck on *Archelon,* the turtle.

There were about 20 different kinds of mosasaurs. Their fossils have been found all over the world in the subtropical seas of the Late Cretaceous period. They probably swam the surface of the sea, occasionally diving for their dinner.

A great many mosasaurs have been found preserved, showing many fine details of the animal's anatomy. There has never been a mosasaur found with babies preserved inside its body. This fact has led mosasaur specialists to conclude that it did not give birth to live offspring in the sea but came ashore to lay eggs. It must have been a spectacular sight to see a 20-foot (a little more than six meters) female mosasaur crawling out of the water on her flippers, looking for a hidden riverbank site or a protected cove to lay her eggs.

The mosasaurs lived with the plesiosaurs (see pages 26–29) and competed with them for food, as the ichthyosaurs (see pages 26–29) had done before they became extinct.

The mosasaurs were most abundant during Late Cretaceous time. Like so many other reptiles, they suddenly became extinct and left no descendants.

Dolphin

Ichthyosaur

Ichthyosaur Skeleton

Plesiosaurs and Ichthyosaurs

There were other groups of reptiles, as well as the lizards, that went back to the sea. They changed in different ways for their new life in the ocean. Their bodies became more streamlined, and their arms and legs developed into fishlike fins. These changes helped them to become excellent swimmers. In spite of the changes you can still recognize these creatures as reptiles.

Ichthyosaurs (IK-thee-o-sawrs, "fish-lizards") first appeared at the end of the Triassic period. They lived into the Jurassic and Cretaceous periods, when they became extinct, along with other seagoing reptiles and dinosaurs. Ichthyosaurs looked like present-day dolphins, porpoises, and small whales. They grew to about 10 or more feet (three or more meters) long and even swam like dolphins, using their flexible bodies and tails to propel them through the water.

The skeleton of an ichthyosaur was once found in Germany with tiny ichthyosaur skeletons inside its abdomen. Some people thought that the large ichthyosaur had eaten the smaller ones. But when the little skeletons were examined carefully by scientists, they found that none of the bones had been crushed, which is what you would expect to happen if a large ichthyosaur had been feeding on its smaller kin. The bones were in perfect condition and were not even partly digested by the stomach juices of the large ichthyosaur. How, then, did the small ichthyosaurs get trapped in the big one? The answer is that they didn't get trapped; they were babies. The pregnant ichthyosaur died before its babies were born. This unique fossil discovery shows that ichthyosaurs, unlike most reptiles, gave birth inside their bodies instead of in eggs outside their bodies. They were born in the sea just as whales are today.

Another group of sea reptiles are the plesiosaurs (PLEEZ-ee-o-sawrs, "almost lizard"). They lived at the same time as the ichthyosaurs but adapted to the sea in a different way. The plesiosaur had a thick, compact body to which a short tail was attached. Added to this basic plan was a small head and a very long, snaky neck, or a short neck and a very large head.

These creatures did not swim in the sea by using powerful strokes of the tail like the ichthyosaurs. They rowed with their arms and legs, which looked like giant paddles, much like the seagoing turtles of today. The arms and legs had become enlarged, and the number of bones in each finger had increased so that in some cases there were 12 joints in each finger. How many joints do you have in your fingers? You have two in your thumb and three in the rest of your fingers.

The earlier plesiosaurs grew to about 10 feet (about three meters) in length, but some of the later ones became giants more than 40 feet (over 12 meters) long. In one group of long-necked plesiosaurs there are as many as 76 neck bones. Because of its long neck this type of plesiosaur is sometimes called swan-lizard.

Some of the plesiosaurs with short necks and giant heads also grew to enormous size. One found in Australia was about 40 feet (over 12 meters) long. It must have been a terrifying monster, with its 10-foot (about three meters) skull and jaws studded with numerous teeth. It was the possessor of the largest reptile skull known.

Another group of aquatic reptiles related to the plesiosaurs is represented by *Placodus* (PLAK-o-dus, ''plate tooth''). Its diet did not consist of fish, as did that of many of the other aquatic reptiles. Instead, it scoured the bottom of the sea floor, searching for and eating all kinds of shellfish. Clams were its main diet.

Placodus had a short neck and tail and paddle-like limbs, which it used to propel itself along the bottom of the sea. It had a protective covering of bony armor, especially thick on its back. As it searched the sea floor, somewhat like a turtle, *Placodus* would snatch up clams with its front teeth. Its powerful jaws had flat-topped teeth with which it crushed the shells. *Placodus* and its relatives lived during the Triassic period. They became extinct before the Jurassic time began.

Plesiosaurus

Placodus

Ichthyosaurus

Plesiosaurus

Plesiosaurus and Ichthyosaurus

Plesiosaurs and ichthyosaurs lived together in many oceans of the world. Shown here is one of the long-necked, small-headed types known as *Plesiosaurus*. As it propelled its way through the sea with its paddlelike limbs, much the way a sea turtle does today, its long neck darted back and forth as it looked for food. When a fish came in range, the snaky head shot out, and the fish was snapped up in jaws that were full of pointed teeth. *Plesiosaurus*' diet consisted of small fish and other swimming animals. It probably even ate pterosaurs that came too close to the ocean surface looking for fish and within range of the hungry jaws of *Plesiosaurus*.

Some plesiosaurs have even been fossilized with their last meal. Found with the stomach contents were small stones that *Plesiosaurus* picked up on the sea floor. These stones had been swallowed and were used to help grind up the food and make it more digestible. Hundreds of these stones have been found in a fossil plesiosaur. The stones are called gastroliths (which means "stomach stones"). They have a dull surface, caused by the digestive juices etching away the rock surface.

Ichthyosaurus was fishlike, able to swim at high speeds. It grew to be about 10 feet (about three meters) long. Its limbs were very small and were used for quick stopping and fast turning. Its eyes were large and its nostrils high on the head, great aids to animals hunting food at the surface of the ocean. Its numerous sharp teeth were long and pointed and set into long grooves in its jaws.

The ichthyosaurs died out before the plesiosaurs, which experienced the same fate several million years later. Just as the extinction of these creatures is a mystery, so is the puzzle of where they came from. They appeared on the scene fully developed. From their internal anatomy it can be determined that they evolved from the cotylosaurs. When, where, and how they did is still unknown, but as more and more fossils are discovered and studied we may be able to find out eventually.

Erythrosuchus

Thecodonts

A group of reptiles evolved during the end of the Permian period with a characteristic that set them apart from most other reptiles. They had teeth that were set in deep sockets in the jaw instead of just being fused to the jaw. These reptiles are called the thecodonts (THEEK-o-donts, ''socket teeth'').

Thecodonts evolved during the Triassic period into a variety of groups. Perhaps this came about because the therapsids had begun to die out at the end of the Permian period. The thecodonts became the more dominant animals. The original thecodonts were waterbound but eventually developed into a branch that could move on land. Both land and waterbound thecodonts generally had front limbs that were shorter than their hind limbs.

Before they became extinct, near the end of the Triassic period, these small thecodonts gave rise to many different types of reptiles. From them came the flying reptiles, the water-loving crocodiles, and the largest of all land animals, the dinosaurs.

In fact, the dinosaurs probably contributed to the extinction of the thecodonts. Dinosaurs and thecodonts both sought the same food, and the thecodonts lost the competition.

All four groups—dinosaurs, thecodonts, crocodiles, and flying reptiles—are called archosaurs (AR-co-sawrs, ''ruling reptiles''). Some scientists include birds as archosaurs.

Erythrosuchus (a-ree-throw-SOOK-us, ''red crocodile,'' is best known from Early Triassic rocks of South Africa. Although a water-dweller, it was probably able to spend some time on land. It was a clumsy-looking creature, with a massive head and a short, heavily built body. Its legs were short and thick, too. It had a mouthful of sharp teeth that were used to dispatch the vegetarian therapsids. *Erythrosuchus* got to be about 10 feet (about three meters) long and weighed as much as 600 pounds (about 275 kilograms).

Desmatosuchus (des-mat-o-SOOK-us, ''linked-to-the-crocodile '') is an unusual-looking thecodont from the Late Triassic period of North America. It developed an unusual coat of armor with hornlike projections. Perhaps the spikes were used for protection. *Desmatosuchus* was short-legged. Its armored body made it extremely heavy.

Desmatosuchus

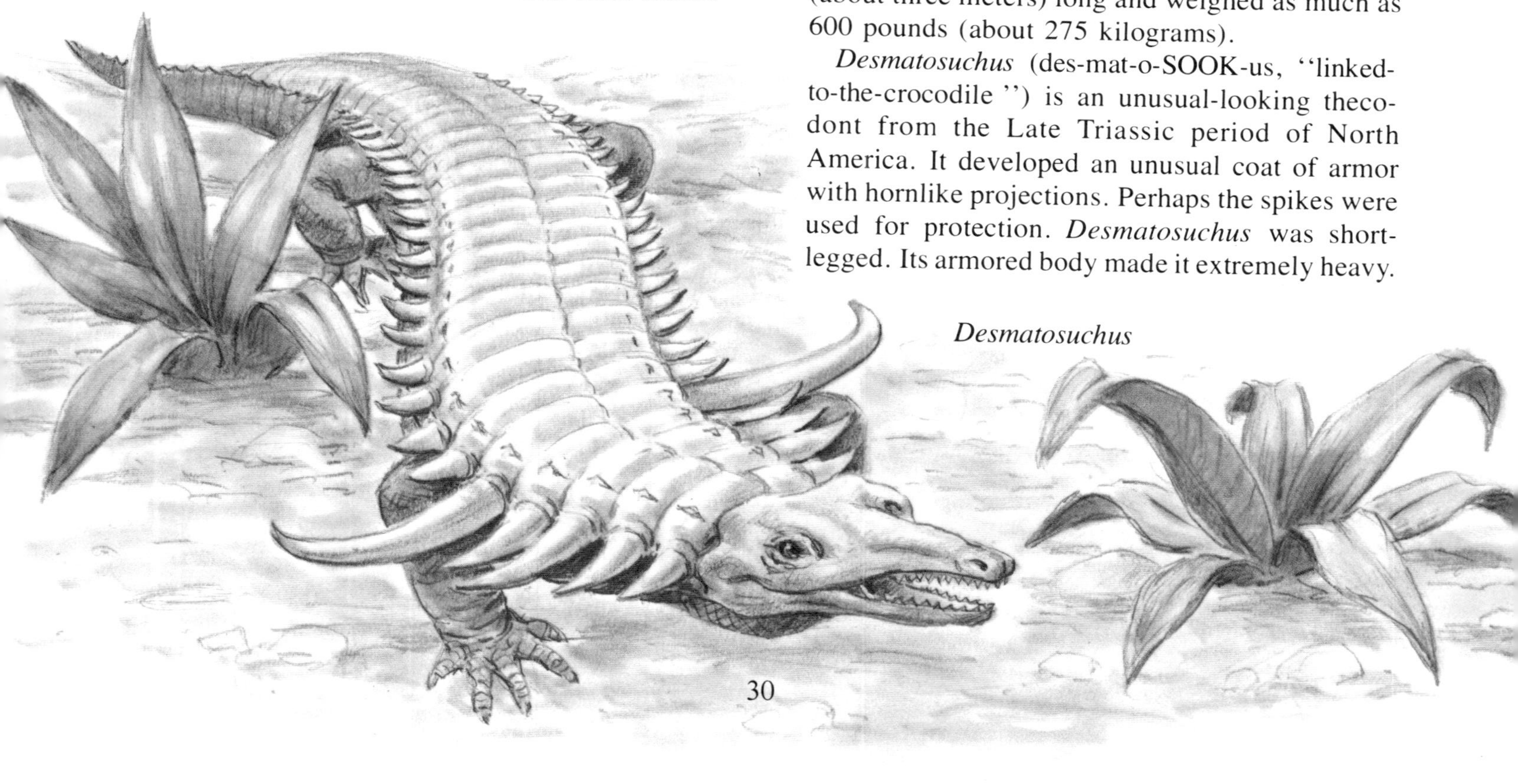

Euparkeria

Its piglike snout and blunt teeth suggest that it dug through the soil looking for roots and other kinds of underground vegetation. It grew up to 20 feet (a little over six meters) long and looked like a crocodile.

One of the earliest land-dwelling thecodonts is known as *Euparkeria* (you-park-ER-ee-ya), named after W. K. Parker, a scientist. This little reptile grew to be five feet (about one and one half meters) long and weighed about 40 pounds (about 18 kilograms). Its fossilized skeletons have been found in South Africa. As you can see in the illustration, *Euparkeria* had hind legs that were much longer than its front limbs. Studies of its anatomy suggest that when *Euparkeria* walked along the ground slowly, it did so on all four legs. But when it was chasing or being chased, it was able to raise itself on its two strong hind legs. Its lightly constructed skeleton allowed *Euparkeria* to run very fast. When it ran, its strong, long tail was used to balance its body. *Euparkeria* used its freed hands to grab and hold an animal while its sharp teeth put its struggling victim to a swift death.

During Triassic time another group of swamp- and marsh-dwelling thecodonts arose that looked and behaved very much like crocodiles. They were called phytosaurs (FYE-toe-sawrs, "plant lizards"). They were given that name because at the time they were discovered it was thought they were plant-eaters. But they were very much the opposite, chasing their prey through swamp waters and using their long, crocodilelike tails to move through the water. They ate fish and any small amphibians or reptiles that came near their long, tooth-filled jaws. One late type found in North America, Europe, and Asia is called *Rutiodon* (ROOT-ee-o-don, "plant tooth"). It could move about on land as well as in the water with its strong legs. *Rutiodon* differed in many ways from crocodiles. For example, *Rutiodon*'s nostrils were in front of the eyes and raised slightly above the top of the head. In crocodiles, the nostrils are in front of the elongated nose. The phytosaurs did not live beyond the Triassic period.

Rutiodon

Birds

In 1861 there was great excitement among the quarrymen around the town of Solnhofen in Bavaria, Germany. The workmen had just discovered a new fossil. This one was different from the other rare and interesting fossils the quarrymen were familiar with in this area. They were always on the lookout for new fossils in the blocks of Late Jurassic limestone that were being removed from the quarries.

They had discovered a dinosaur, but not an ordinary dinosaur. This one had feathers on one of the arms and pairs of feathers on most of the tail vertebrae.

Because it had feathers it was surely a bird. It was named *Archaeopteryx* (ar-kee-OP-ter-ix, "ancient wing"). Since that time four more skeletons have been found. One of these fossils lay misidentified for many years in a museum. It was thought to be a dinosaur. The feathers were so lightly preserved that they were difficult to see.

Archaeopteryx is a primitive bird, though many of its features were more reptilian than birdlike. *Archaeopteryx* belongs somewhere in the middle of the change from dinosaur to bird. If you want to see a clue to the reptilian origin of birds, take a

Archaeopteryx

good look at a chicken's feet. They are scaly, like reptile skin. Feathers originated as modified reptile scales.

Recent detailed studies show that *Archaeopteryx* is very much like its ancestor, a theropod dinosaur. These studies conclude that it could not fly and probably could not even glide. We know now that feathers are an important part of a bird's flying equipment. Why, then, did *Archaeopteryx* have feathers if it couldn't fly?

To answer this question we have to see what *Archaeopteryx* was really like. It was a fast-moving, meat-eating animal, just like the small dinosaurs it evolved from. It was the size of a crow and used its jaws and teeth to catch large insects, lizards, and maybe even small mammals. Perhaps its feathers first developed to help protect its body against heat and cold so that eventually its descendants became warm-blooded creatures. As *Archaeopteryx* used its feathered arms to beat down and grasp its prey, the usefulness of feathers as a means of making movement quicker and easier may have gradually developed into flight.

Quetzalcoatlus

Pterosaurs

Some archosaurs (''ruling reptiles'') took to the air. It is possible that the pterosaurs (tair-O-sawrs, ''winged lizards'') developed from warm-blooded, tree-living thecodonts.

These thecodonts may have been able to glide from tree to tree with the help of a flap of skin that stretched between the abdomen and the long arms and fourth finger.

We really do not know how pterosaurs spent their resting time. Their in-turned feet were not designed for walking or resting on the ground. One guess is that they hung suspended, batlike, from trees or cliffs near their ocean homes.

Rhamphorhynchus (ram-fo-RINK-us, ''prow beak'') is an example of the early type of pterosaur. As with birds, its bones were light because they were filled with air.

Rhamphorhynchus had many sharp teeth in its jaws. Its wings and head were large in relationship to its body Its wingspan was about three feet (about one meter) and, like all pterosaurs, it was able to fly and glide on air currents. *Rhamphorhynchus* had a long tail. Attached to the tip of the tail was a small rudder to help it steer. It probably scooped fish from the ocean with its jaws as it swooped low over the water.

The rhamphorhynchoids became extinct at the end of the Jurassic period. From them evolved the pterodactyls (tair-o-DAK-tils, ''winged finger'') during the middle of the Jurassic. One of the pterodactyls, *Pteranodon* (tair-AN-o-don), had wings but no teeth. It lived during Late Cretaceous time in what is now Kansas. Its largest wingspan was about 25 feet (about eight meters) and it may have weighed as much as 150 pounds (about 68 kilograms).

No one is certain about the purpose of the long, bony crest on top of its skull. One suggestion is that it acted as a balance for the long, toothless jaws. Other pterodactyls did not have these peculiar crests. Not all of the pterodactyls were large. The earlier forms were as small as robins.

Quetzalcoatlus (kwet-sole-CO-at-lus, ''Aztec feathered serpent god'') was the largest pterosaur and the largest flying creature that ever lived. It was found in Late Cretaceous rocks in Big Bend National Park, Texas. It had a wingspan of 50 feet (a little more than 15 meters). Its skull and jaws were long and thin, and its long neck and head probably had a length of eight or nine feet (about two and one half meters).

Can you picture this furry creature taking a few wobbly leaps over the ground and flapping its wings back and forth, trying to take off? Once up, *Quetzalcoatlus* caught rising hot air currents that took it high into the air. There it glided over the landscape, occasionally flapping its giant wings to take it into a new air current.

What did *Quetzalcoatlus* eat? Studies indicate that *Quetzalcoatlus* was the vulture of its day, living off dead animals—and these dead animals were most likely dinosaurs.

Therefore it is possible that *Quetzalcoatlus* became extinct because its food source disappeared and there was nothing to replace it at the time.

We really don't know why the other pterosaurs died out. Perhaps birds were better at getting food than the pterosaurs. If this is true, the pterosaurs may have been starved into extinction.

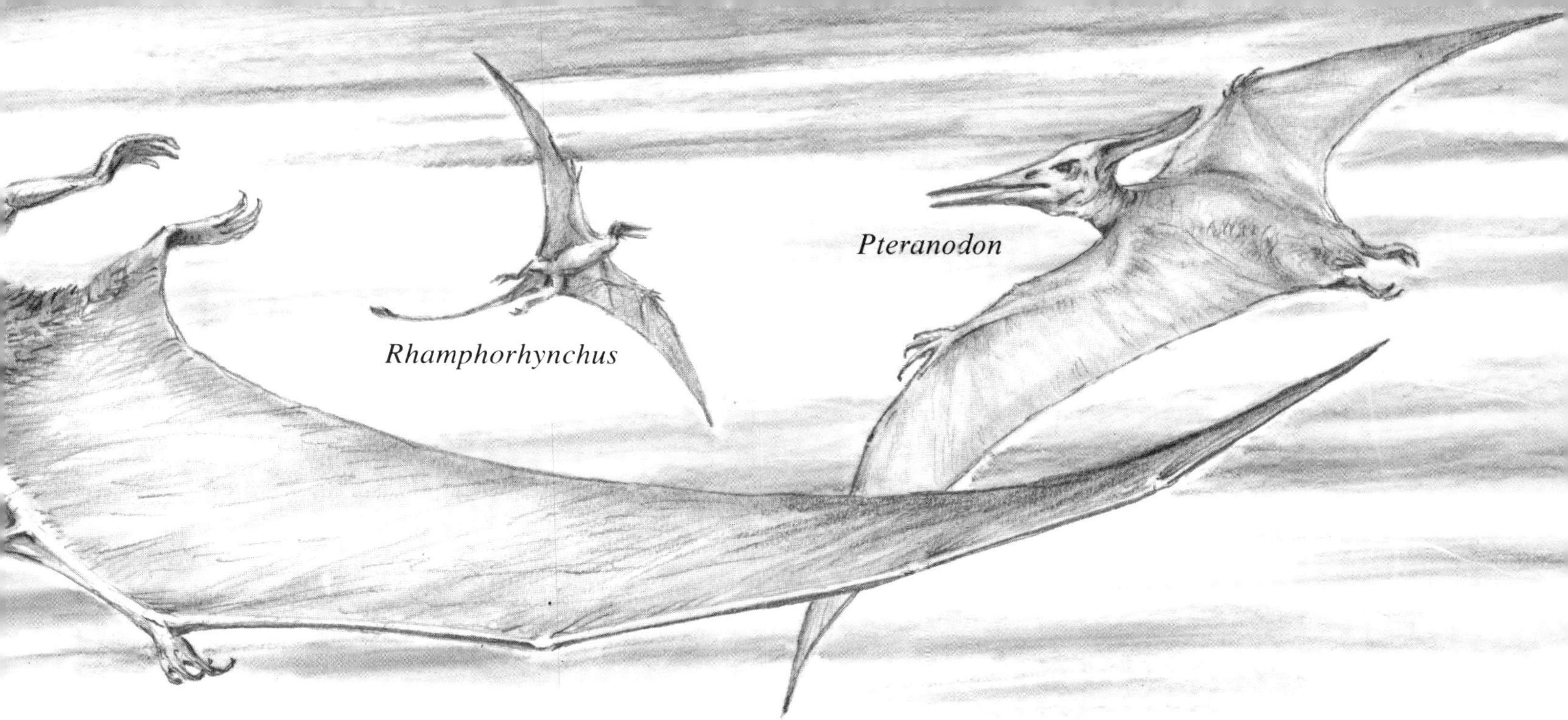

Pteranodon

Rhamphorhynchus

Crocodiles

Crocodiles and birds are the closest living relatives of the dinosaurs, though usually we do not think of birds as reptiles because they do not look like reptiles and they have feathers.

The fossil record of crocodiles is nearly 200 million years long, going back to the Middle Triassic period. Crocodiles evolved from thecodonts that were mainly marsh-dwelling reptiles. Some of the early crocodiles adapted to living on dry land, but they did not survive very long. Competition for food with small dinosaurs caused their extinction. Only the marsh- and swamp-dwellers survived.

Protosuchus (pro-toe-SOOK-us, "first crocodile") is one of the early land-dwelling crocodiles. It lived during Late Triassic time in Arizona. *Protosuchus* had the sharp teeth of a meat-eater and a double row of bony ridges on its back to give it some protection from other meat-eaters. It also had strong legs for walking on land.

The early water-dwelling crocodiles competed for food with the phytosaurs. Unlike those of the phytosaurs, the nostrils of the crocodiles are at the tip of their long, thin jaws. The nostrils are completely separated from the mouth so that the crocodiles can chew and bite under water without drowning. Crocodiles have survived to this day, while phytosaurs became extinct at the end of the Triassic period.

The next geologic period, the Jurassic, saw an expansion of the crocodile family into a great variety of types. They also entered new living areas, such as the mouths of large rivers and even the ocean.

Like so many other animals that became ocean dwellers, the crocodiles also changed form as they became more and more adapted to ocean life. One of these ocean dwellers, *Geosaurus* (jee-o-SAWR-us, "earth lizard") was about 15 feet (about four and a half meters) long. The arms and legs took the form of paddles, the tail became fin-like, and the bony, armorlike skin, which is typical of the crocodiles, was lost. *Geosaurus* became extinct during the Early Cretaceous period and was succeeded in the food chain by the mosasaurs. (See pages 24–25.)

Protosuchus

Geosaurus

Dinosaurs—What Are They?

The name dinosaur (DINE-o-sawr) means "terrible lizard." However, most dinosaurs were not terrible but full of surprises. Some dinosaurs were so enormous and so different from any animal alive today that they excite the imagination. They varied a great deal in size and shape—from tiny creatures little bigger than a chicken to 60-ton (about 54,500 kilograms) plant-eating, gentle giants to scaly, spiked, monstrous carnivores.

It is surprising how little we know about them. For example, there is disagreement among the dinosaur specialists about which thecodonts are the dinosaurs' ancestors. Some of these scientists believe that dinosaurs evolved from one branch. Others believe that different groups of dinosaurs came from different groups of thecodonts. There is even doubt about the origin of the thecodonts. Most scientists believe that the thecodonts evolved from the cotylosaurs.(See pages 15–17.)Others see them evolving from the pelycosaurs (pages 18–19). It seems that the more we learn about thecodonts the less we know about dinosaur origins.

Reptiles living today are cold-blooded. Some scientists believe that dinosaurs, however, may have been special reptiles that were warm-blooded. Here again there are very different points of view. The indirect evidence for or against any theory is difficult to prove.

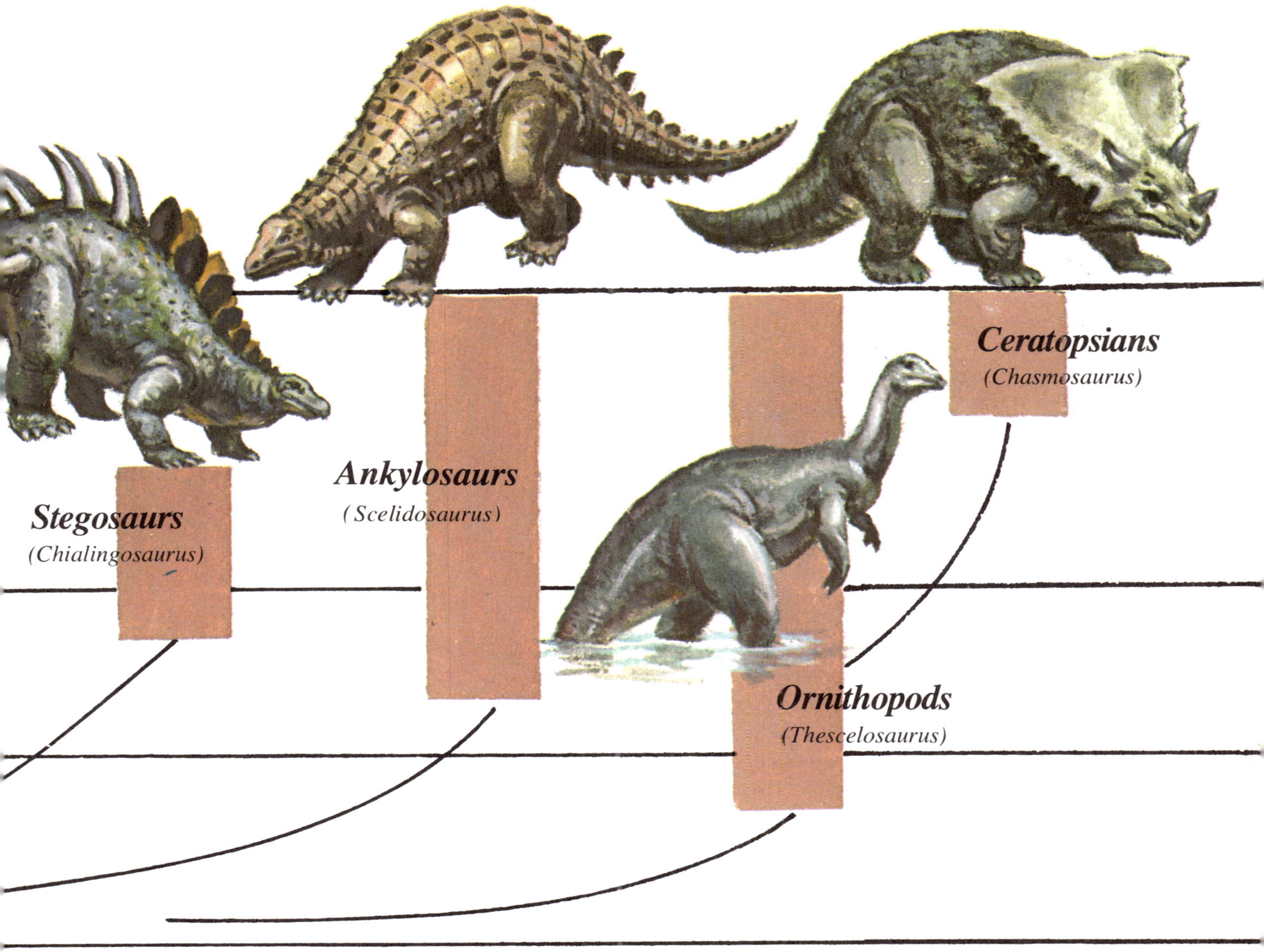

One thing we know is that dinosaurs fall into clearly defined groups based on the difference in the pelvic, or hip, bones.

The saurischians (sawr-ISS-kee-ans, ''lizard pelvis'') and the ornithischians (or-nith-ISS-kee-ans, ''bird pelvis'') are the two main groupings.

When you go to a museum take this book with you. Compare the hip bones of the dinosaur with the illustration in the chart. You will be able to tell if the dinosaur is a saurischian or an ornithischian.

The saurischians are divided into two groups: the theropods (thair-o-PODES, ''beast feet'') and the sauropodamorphs (sawr-o-PODE-a-morfs, ''lizard-foot form'').

The ornithischians are subdivided into the ornithopods (or-NITH-o-pods, ''bird foot''), stegosaurs (STEG-o-sawrs, ''covered lizards''), ankylosaurs (an-KILE-o-sawrs, ''curved lizards''), and ceratopsians (sair-a-TOP-see-ans, ''horn faces'').

The theropods are the only dinosaurs that were meat-eaters. All the others were plant-eaters. The theropods and ornithopods walked on two feet. All the rest of them were four-footed.

The diagram shows examples of each group. The thick lines show when the groups lived. The thin lines show how the groups may have been related. The relationship is one of many guesses.

Theropods

Coelophysis (SEE-lo-fise-iss, "hollow nature") was a Late Triassic dinosaur that looked like the thecodont *Euparkeria* (page 31). It was eight or nine feet (about two and one half meters) long, light-boned, and weighed about 60 pounds (about 27 kilograms). It had a smaller head than *Euparkeria* and many sharp teeth, typical of a carnivore. Its neck was more flexible, and its longer hind legs equipped it for fast running.

The legs of *Coelophysis* were birdlike, like many of the dinosaurs. It had five toes but only three of them were used for walking. When it walked on wet ground it left tracks that looked like the footprints of a bird.

Coelophysis and its relatives were found on all continents. They lasted to the end of the Cretaceous period, making them the longest-lived dinosaur group.

This group produced dinosaurs that were very birdlike in appearance. If you removed their reptilian tails they would seem like ostriches. In fact, they are called the ostrich dinosaurs. They had long legs, thin arms, and small heads.

Ornithomimus (or-nith-o-MIME-us, "bird imitator") was a birdlike dinosaur that lived during the Cretaceous period in North America and Asia.

One of the unusual features of this dinosaur was that it didn't have teeth. What did it eat? What diet can you think of for a dinosaur that had hands that couldn't pick up or hold things, who was toothless, and fast-moving?

One theory is that it was a nest robber. It would sneak up on an unattended dinosaur nest and steal an egg, break it with its beaky jaw and suck out the contents. If it was caught in the act, it could speed away on its fast feet.

Of course, we don't know if this is the way it got its food. We don't even know if all dinosaurs laid eggs. We do know a few of them did because we have found their fossilized eggs. And one of the egg-laying dinosaurs did live at the same time as *Ornithomimus*.

Ornithomimus could have just as easily eaten fruits and berries, or even frogs and salamanders. No teeth are needed to devour these foods.

Deinonychus (DIE-no-ni-kuss, "terrible claw") is another small dinosaur. It was also about eight

Deinonychus

Coelophysis

Ornithomimus

Allosaurus

feet (a little under two and one half meters) long, built a little more heavily than *Coelophysis*. It probably weighed as much as an average woman (about 125 pounds or 57 kilograms).

This little meat-eater lived in Montana and Wyoming during the Early Cretaceous period. It had large claws on its front and hind feet. It is easy to imagine *Deinonychus* leaping onto the back of a large herbivore. Being more agile, the meat-eater could easily disable the giant with the help of its deadly claws and sharp teeth.

Compared to its body, *Deinonychus* had a larger head than we have seen in many of the other reptiles. The big skull, jaw, and teeth, combined with a large, powerful bipedal body, is typical of carnosaurs (CAR-no-sawrs, "meat-lizard"), the group of large, meat-eating giants that flourished during the Jurassic and Cretaceous periods. *Megalosaurus* (page 36), *Tyrannosaurus* (tie-RAN-o-sawr-us, "tyrant lizard," illustrated on page 41), and *Allosaurus* (AL-o-sawr-us, "other lizard") were among the largest carnivores that ever lived on the land.

Megalosaurus was about 20 feet (a little over six meters) in length and weighed about 2,000 pounds (about 910 kilograms). Many bone fragments and teeth from almost every part of the world have been identified as *Megalosaurus*, making it seem as if *Megalosaurus* ranged in age from Jurassic to Cretaceous time. However, many of the bones and teeth may have been misidentified and may belong to other dinosaurs whose teeth are similar.

Megalosaurus has the honor of being the first dinosaur to be described scientifically. It lived in England during the Early Jurassic period. It had a typical large head, big mouth, and many sharp teeth. Its long tail balanced its head as it moved through the landscape searching for food.

Allosaurus, also known as *Antrodemus* (an-troe-DEE-mus, "hollow build"), was even larger. It grew to a length of 30 feet (over nine meters) and weighed as much as 10,000 pounds (4,550 kilograms). Many skeletons have been found in Late Jurassic rocks of the western United States.

Even though it was a large animal it could run fast on its extremely strong legs. Its clawed feet and small arms were used to hold down a victim as its huge teeth tore large pieces of flesh from the body. *Allosaurus* would then gulp down the huge chunks of unchewed meat.

Tyrannosaurus

Of all the carnosaurs, *Tyrannosaurus* was king. It grew to a length of 50 feet (a little over 15 meters) and weighed 20,000 pounds (about 9,100 kilograms). Its head stood 20 feet (a little over six meters) off the ground when it wasn't running. When it did run its head stretched out in front of its body and it lifted its tail off the ground.

The head of *Tyrannosaurus* was more than four feet (a little over one meter) long. It had about 60 teeth in its mouth, and some of them were six inches (about 15 centimeters) long. The teeth were serrated just like the steak knives in your kitchen. This, as you know, makes for easier cutting. All of the teeth curved toward the back of the mouth so that the food could be more easily swallowed.

The huge chunks that were swallowed were probably ground up in the stomach with the aid of rounded rocks called gastroliths—"stomach stones." It is possible that all the carnivorous dinosaurs used rocks to help them digest their food. It is said that one bite by *Tyrannosaurus* could supply a human family of four with meat for a month.

The hands of *Tyrannosaurus* were very small, as you can see in the illustration. They could just

touch each other. There were only two clawed fingers on each hand. Turn back the page and compare the hands with those of *Allosaurus*. What do you think *Tyrannosaurus* used its hands for? Many people believe that they were useless. Did they have a special use that we do not know about? What if *Tyrannosaurus* did not sleep standing up but on its side on the ground? (We don't know how they slept.) It could have used its hands to help it get off the ground. What do you think?

Tyrannosaurus had many relatives that looked just like it during the Late Cretaceous period. In Asia, the carnosaurs look so much like *Tyrannosaurus* that they could be misidentified by scientists if they were not told where the specimens came from. This close identity is further proof that Mongolia and the western United States were once connected by a continuous strip of land. *Tyrannosaurus* was a terrestrial animal, so you wouldn't expect *Tyrannosaurus* to swim the ocean. The Cretaceous world looked different from the way it does today. Continents were in different places and had different shapes. The Cretaceous land connection is in the area of today's Alaska and Russia.

Sauropodamorphs

The sauropodamorphs (sawr-o-PODE-a-morfs, "lizard-foot forms") evolved into the largest creatures that ever roamed the land. Their origin, like that of so many other animal groups, is only guessed at.

Some scientists believe that these quadrupedal (four-footed) giants evolved from a bipedal (two-footed) thecodont. The thecodont itself evolved from a quadrupedal thecodont. The sauropodamorph ancestors were bipedal with short front limbs. During their evolution these legs got longer and longer but not as long as the hind legs. Almost all of these animals had front legs that were shorter than the hind legs.

Another theory is that the longer hind legs evolved to help carry most of the animal's weight, which was in the rear. The front of the animal had less weight and, therefore, did not need legs that were as long.

The earliest four-legged sauropodamorphs evolved from a reptile that could have looked like *Erythrosuchus* (page 30) during the end of the Early Triassic period. These early four-legged types lived in swamps and marshes. During the Triassic period they evolved into a variety of types. Some remained four-legged; others became two-legged. Some were meat-eaters, and others were plant-eaters.

All of these early sauropodamorphs became extinct at the end of the Triassic period. One group, however, gave rise to the Jurassic and Cretaceous giants called sauropods.

Plateosaurus (PLATE-ee-o-sawr-us, "flat lizard") is one of these Triassic sauropodamorphs. Its skeleton has been found in South Africa and Germany in rocks that formed during the Late Triassic period. Skeletons of *Plateosaurus* are about 20 feet (a little more than six meters) long. Its front legs were shorter than its hind legs. Like some other dinosaurs, *Plateosaurus* was probably both bipedal and quadrupedal, depending on its activity. If it moved slowly, it moved about on four legs. But if it ran, it did so on two legs. Examination of *Plateosaurus* teeth shows that they were meat-eaters, and they were not in the ancestral line that gave rise to the sauropods.

Diplodocus

Apatosaurus
Brontosaurus

Plateosaurus

The giant Jurassic and Cretaceous sauropods have excited the imagination of everyone from the first moment that they were discovered. They had long necks and tails and relatively small bodies. One scientist describes a sauropod as having the neck of a giraffe, the limbs of an elephant, clawed feet, the lungs of a bird, the tail of a lizard, and maybe a tiny, trunklike nose. All of the sauropods seem to look the same because of their giant size.

Apatosaurus (a-PAT-o-sawr-us, "deceptive lizard"), also known as *Brontosaurus* (BRON toe-sawr-us, "thunder lizard"), lived during the Late Jurassic period in the western United States. It weighed 70,000 pounds (about 31,800 kilograms) and reached a length of 75 feet (23 meters).

These creatures must have done a lot of damage to the forest trees and to slow-moving animals as they came thundering through. Imagine the stir if they moved in herds!

Diplodocus (di-PLOD-ok-us, "double beam") also lived during the Late Jurassic period. It grew to a length of 90 feet (a little over 27½ meters), making it the longest land animal that ever lived. It was not as heavily built as *Apatosaurus* and therefore weighed much less. Can you imagine how much food it had to eat every day? Its mouth was small compared to its body. It probably had to eat continuously.

Cetiosaurus (page 36) was smaller, about 45 feet (a little under eight and one half meters) long, and its head was about 20 feet (a little over six meters) off the ground. It weighed about 20,000 pounds, or 10 tons (about 9,100 kilograms).

How long did these giants live? Reptiles, unlike mammals, continue to grow all their lives. When they are older they do not grow as fast. Did these giants live for hundreds and hundreds of years until they were killed by disease, accident or carnivores? Nobody knows the answer.

Brachiosaurus

Brachiosaurus (BRACK-ee-o-sawr-us, ''arm lizard'') was the heaviest sauropod of all. You would have to go to a museum in Berlin, Germany, to see its skeleton. The skeleton was found in Tanzania, Africa. It is 40 feet (a little more than 12 meters) tall. The upper bone in its leg alone is taller than an average man. *Brachiosaurus* also lived in the United States and Europe during the Late Jurassic period. *Brachiosaurus* has been estimated to weigh 85 tons (about 77,300 kilograms) when it was alive and was 75 feet (23 meters) long. That is more than twice the weight of *Apatosaurus* or more than 12 of the largest elephants put together. Today, the only animals that are larger—the blue whales—live in the ocean and can weigh 100 tons (about 91,000 kilograms) and more.

The front legs of *Brachiosaurus* were slightly longer than its rear legs. This is one of the differences between it and its relatives. It looked a little like a giraffe, being taller at the shoulder than at the hips.

The leaves from the tops of trees that lined the numerous rivers were probably an important part of its diet. It had a small head and the peglike teeth typical of plant-eaters. Its brain was about the size of an orange.

The illustration shows a *Brachiosaurus* feeding on the land and another one partly submerged in water. We don't really know whether these huge creatures lived on land or in the water or spent some time in both environments.

Some scientists believe *Brachiosaurus* and the other giants were so large that they couldn't support their huge bodies on the land. They believe the heart would not have been able to pump blood to the top of the head if it was held erect like a giraffe's. They may have lived in water, where most of their weight would be supported by the water.

Other scientists believe that their limbs were strong enough to support their great weight and that there was no problem getting blood to the head.

Unfortunately there are no living animals today that can be compared to *Brachiosaurus* or any of its relatives.

Although we have its bones, there is really very little we know about the way it lived. It probably lived near water and was a vegetarian. Its long neck could have been used for browsing on trees, or maybe even under water in lakes and rivers.

It may have been able to rear up on its hind legs. It probably walked around with its tail off the ground but occasionally dragged it. It could have used its tail for striking its enemies.

Large animals were probably not bothered by carnivores like *Antrodemus*. These ferocious killers probably attacked and killed individuals that were its own size or smaller.

Brachiosaurus

Corythosaurus

Ornithopods

All of the bipedal ornithischians are members of the ornithopods. The earliest ornithopod was found in Argentina in rocks that date from the early part of the Late Triassic period. They evolved into a great variety of animals and were very common during the Late Jurassic and Early Cretaceous periods.

Hypsilophodon (hip-si-LOFE-o-don, "high-crested tooth") is a member of a family of ornithopods that has been pictured in the past as a tree climber. These animals grew to five or six feet (less than two meters) in length; they had five fingers and four toes. Recent studies of these primitive ornithopods indicate that they were highly adapted for fast running. Running ability was one of the features of the early ornithopods.

Kritosaurus

Another small Early Cretaceous ornithopod is *Psittacosaurus* (sit-a-co-SAWR-us, "parrot-lizard"). Like most of the ornithopods, it had no teeth at the front of the mouth. As its name suggests it had a parrotlike beak that was used for food gathering. It is this feature, among others, that makes scientists think *Psittacosaurus* is somewhere in the middle of the line of evolution that leads from the ornithopods to the horned dinosaurs.

Camptosaurus (page 49) and *Iguanodon* (ig-WAN-o-don, illustrated on page 48) are usually thought of as the typical ornithopod dinosaurs. *Camptosaurus* lived during the Late Jurassic period in Wyoming, Utah, England, and France. They may also have lived in South Dakota during the Early Cretaceous and in Transylvania during the Late Cretaceous. Many skeletons have been found in the United States. They range in size from about four feet to 15 feet (over one meter to four and one half meters) in length and could have weighed as much as 1,500 pounds (about 700 kilograms).

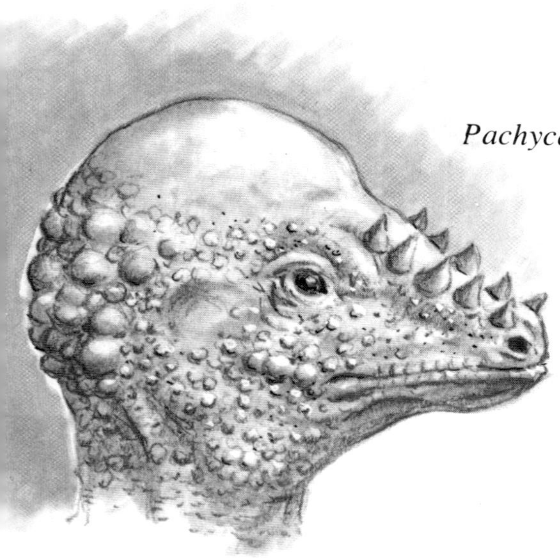

Pachycephalosaurus

Iguanodon is very much like *Camptosaurus*, but it is much larger and has certain features that are not found in *Camptosaurus*.

An unusual ornithopod is called *Pachycephalosaurus* (pak-ee-SEF-a-lo-sawr-us, "thick-headed lizard"). This is a good name for a dinosaur that has a 10-inch- (24 centimeters) thick mass of bone forming the top of its skull. These dinosaurs are also known as dome-heads and bone-heads because of this feature. The illustration shows why.

What purpose do you think the bone had? One guess is that these dinosaurs used their "domes" for butting each other, the same way as fighting goats do today. These dinosaurs were found in western North America. They lived during the Late Cretaceous period.

A group related to bone-heads were called the hadrosaurs (HAD-roe-saurs, "bulk lizards"). They are also called the duckbill dinosaurs. As you can see below, the shape of the head and the jaws was broad and flat. As in the ornithopods in general, the jaws were toothless up front, but at the back of the jaws hadrosaurs could have as many as 2,000 teeth. These teeth were used for grinding vegetation. As individual teeth were worn away, they fell out and were replaced with new ones. These amphibious ornithopods lived on land and in shallow lakes, rivers, and the sea during the Late Cretaceous period in Europe, Asia, and North America.

Mummies of these hadrosaurs have been discovered. In mummies, the skin of the animal is preserved, showing features that are not found in fossilized bones. Their hands looked as if they were covered with mittens and their feet were webbed; the tail was like a crocodile's. All of these features are useful for a creature that spends some time in water. They were probably good swimmers.

One hadrosaur mummy has its stomach contents preserved. The contents consist of conifers, willows, and oaks. Not only were the leaves eaten but also the twigs and other hard plant parts. Perhaps the animals lived near the edge of water bodies, feeding in the nearby forests. In time of danger they could jump into the river or lake and swim away.

The skeletons of all the different kinds of hadrosaurs were similar except for the head. Their heads developed into a wide variety of shapes. They are classified into two groups, the flat-headed and crest hadrosaurs.

Parasaurolophus (pair-a-sawr-OL-o-fus, "close to lizard crest") shows the general form of the hadrosaur body. This crested hadrosaur had a hollow tube that projected from the top of the skull. It was an enlargement and elongation of the nasal passages.

The head of *Corythosaurus* (kor-ITH-o-sawr-us, "helmet lizard") had a large hollow space under its helmet-shaped head that was connected to its nasal passages.

Kritosaurus (KRITE-o-sawr-us, "chosen lizard") is an example of a flat-headed hadrosaur. Its nasal bones were slightly swollen and formed a bump in front of the eyes.

What purpose did the crests serve? Why didn't all of them have crests? There are many theories but none of them successfully answer these questions. Was the crest used for making loud sounds? Maybe they increased the animal's sense of smell. Or did the crests allow them to stay submerged in water for a long time? Nobody knows for sure.

Parasaurolophus

Iguanodon

Iguanodon was the first fossil animal to be recognized as a reptile. Its teeth were found by the wife of an English doctor in 1822 in Sussex, in the southern part of England. She found the teeth in crushed rock that was being used for repairing a road. The teeth looked very much like those of the present-day vegetable-eating reptile *Iguana*.

Later the rock quarry was located and the bones of the dinosaur were also found.

In 1878, many skeletons of *Iguanodon* were uncovered in Belgium during coal mining. During the Early Cretaceous period, this part of Belgium was a swampy area that also had some drier, hilly areas here and there. Hidden in the lush vegetation were natural pits, some 1,000 feet (about 310 meters) deep. An *Iguanodon* that lost its step might fall over the edge of a pit to its death. With the specimens of *Iguanodon* are found fish, turtles, crocodiles, ferns, and other plants. Later the pits filled up with sediment and the animals and plants were preserved.

With these skeletons and others found before and after, *Iguanodon* has become one of the best-known dinosaurs.

It was a large, bipedal dinosaur that had excellent teeth for grinding up leaves and other plant parts. The strong-looking arms were about half the size of its powerful legs. The legs had four toes, but only three were used for walking. The hands had five fingers, but the thumb was a spike. Why would an animal have a spike for a thumb? No one knows. We can only make guesses. One scientist suggested that the spike was used for defense. Any time an *Allosaurus* or other meat-eater tried to attack, *Iguanodon* would strike out with its spike and hit its opponent right in the eye.

Iguanodon had a long tail that was flattened on the bottom. It is thought that while resting it sat on its hind legs and tail. Although *Iguanodon* could grow to be 30 feet (a little over 9 meters) from the tip of the tail to the tip of its head, its head was probably only about 16 feet (a little under five meters) above the ground.

Iguanodon fossils have been found in many different parts of the earth. In Europe, besides England and Belgium, they have been found also in France, Portugal, and Spain. Footprints that may belong to *Iguanodon* have been found on Spitzbergen Island, only 12 degrees from the North Pole. Related kinds of iguanodons have been found in Mongolia, Africa, Australia, and North America.

The geographic distribution of *Iguanodon* and its relatives shows that these places were all connected by dry land.

Camptosaurus

The Horned Dinosaurs

The ceratopsians, or horned-face dinosaurs, were the last group of dinosaurs to evolve. They may have evolved from the ornithopods. *Psittacosaurus*, a two-legged ornithopod, had a beak that looks like a parrot's.

Protoceratops (pro-to-SAIR-a-tops, "first horn face"), the first known horned dinosaur from the Late Cretaceous period of Mongolia, had a similar parrotlike beak. The similarity makes it seem possible that *Protoceratops* evolved from the ornithopods. If this is so, its ornithopod ancestor must have given up being two-legged and gone down on all fours.

Protoceratops had a fan-shaped bone at the back of the head, covering its neck. This made its head appear larger and also protected its neck from attack. To this large bone were attached the jaw muscles and the muscles that kept the head erect. *Protoceratops* grew to be about six feet (under two meters) long and weighed as much as 900 pounds (409 kilograms).

Some of the best dinosaur eggs ever found were some that belonged to a *Protoceratops*. Many nests have been discovered in Mongolia, fossilized in what looks like desert sand. Not only are there eggs but even some baby *Protoceratops* in the process of hatching out of their eggs. The largest eggs are about nine inches (about 22 centimeters) long; there were about 30 eggs in each nest.

One of the obvious features of the ceratopsians is the fan-shaped bone that extends out from the back of the skull. These bony extensions are called frills. Frills are grouped into short frills and long frills.

The short frills are wide and rounded. They measure about one-third to one-half of the length of the skull. Most of the short frills have openings or holes in them. *Triceratops* (tri-SAIR-a-tops, "three-horn face"), illustrated on pages 52–53, is one of the exceptions. Its frill has no holes. *Monoclonius* (mon-o-KLONE-ee-us, "single stem") has bony bumps around the margins of the frills. *Styracosaurus* was about the same size as *Monoclonius*, 16 to 18 feet (a little less than five meters to a little more than five and one half meters) long.

Protoceratops

Styracosaurus

Monoclonius

Torosaurus

Chasmosaurus

All the long frills are rectangular in outline and all of them have holes. They measured about one-half to two-thirds of the length of the skull. Most of the long-frilled ceratopsians have either bony extensions or indentations on the margins of the frills. *Torosaurus* (TOR-o-sar-us, "piercing lizard") was almost the size of *Triceratops,* and its head, including the frills, was almost half the length of the body. *Torosaurus* was about 25 feet (under eight meters) long. *Chasmosaurus* (see pages 31–32), another long-frilled, horned dinosaur, weighed 8,000 pounds (a little less than 3,650 kilograms) and reached a length of 17 feet (more than five meters).

Unlike many other vegetarian dinosaurs, the ceratopsians had no bony armor to protect themselves against meat-eaters. They did have thick skin, which may have given some protection. But more importantly, most of them had horns. A 25 or 30-foot- (more than seven and one half to more than nine meters) long *Triceratops* would have made an excellent stand against the largest of the meat-eaters.

The horns were a little like those you find on cattle today. As you can see in these illustrations, some ceratopsians had three horns, two over the eyes on the brows and one over the nasal area. In some types, the nasal horn was absent, and in others only the nasal horn was present. *Protoceratops* did not have horns.

Another interesting feature of the ceratopsians were the beaks. They combined some of the features of birds and turtles. The beaks were very narrow like a bird's, and the tips of the beaks curved toward each other like a turtle's. They do not seem to have had sharp edges and therefore could not be used as cutting instruments. Most likely they were used to grasp and pull vegetation from the ground.

Triceratops

The ceratopsians originated at the beginning of Late Cretaceous time in Asia and migrated to North America. The migration was possible because Asia and North America were once connected to each other. This land bridge was, in fact, the last major link between the continents. Less than 150 million years before, all of the continents had been interconnected to form one huge land mass. From that time the land mass has been breaking up into smaller segments. Even this last connection was cut. The break happened after all the dinosaurs were gone. It reappeared for a short time as the Bering Land Bridge between Alaska and Asia, during the Ice Age.

After the first ceratopsians reached North America, they evolved rapidly into many different types. Of all these, *Triceratops* is best known. It is also the largest known ornithischian. It grew to a maximum of 36 feet (11 meters) and probably weighed as much as 20,000 pounds (9,091 kilograms). The tall, pillarlike legs supported the huge body and short, powerful tail. Like all of the ornithischians, its hind legs were longer than its front ones. Its large head took up about one-third of its body.

Studies of the jaw muscles, teeth, and parrotlike beak of *Triceratops* and other ceratopsians show that they could feed on only certain kinds of plants. They didn't have teeth to crush or grind seeds, fruit, or ordinary leaves. The teeth they did have were unlike any other animal's. They were constructed to slice like scissors when they moved past

Triceratops

each other. Their beaks were designed for grabbing and pulling plant material.

The exact diet of these reptiles is unknown, but a scientist who studied these animals thinks that they may have eaten palms and cycads. These were very tough plants that grew close to the ground. The branches came out of the trunk in a circle, making the tree look like a giant, inside-out umbrella. The leafy branches were low enough for the ceratopsians to reach.

Triceratops could, of course, be a substantial meal for meat-eaters like *Tyrannosaurus*. However, it had some protection against attack—the frill around its neck and the three horns on its head. Two of them came out of the skull above the eyes on the forehead and the third from the nasal area.

Triceratops was the last dinosaur to evolve and may have been the last dinosaur to become extinct.

A lot is known about these reptiles because there are many excellently preserved specimens. The changes that appear in them from their first to last occurrence include a general trend to increased size and a shortening of the tail. With increased size there was a shortening of the front and hind legs. The hind legs were affected much more. The development of their special teeth, the horn on the brow or nose, and an increase in the size of the frills were all changes that occurred in the evolution of the ceratopsians.

Kentrosaurus

Stegosaurs

The stegosaurs are the only dinosaurs that became extinct before the end of Cretaceous time. They range from Middle Jurassic to Early Cretaceous. The best preserved skeletons come from the Late Jurassic. Rocks from the other time periods have given us only fragments of these creatures.

The stegosaurs were sluggish, vegetable-eating reptiles that have been found in North America, Europe, Asia, and Africa during the Late Jurassic.

All the stegosaurs were very much the same. *Kentrosaurus* was about 16 feet (a little under five meters) long and had two rows of spikes on its tail and halfway up its back. From the middle of the back toward its neck the spikes were replaced by small plates.

Chialingosaurus (ky-a-ling-o-SAWR-us, named after the Chinese river Chialing) is very similar to *Kentrosaurus*. It is from the Upper Jurassic of China. The similarity of all these animals is due to the close connections that they had to one another when all of the continents were nearly joined together.

Stegosaurus (STEG-o-sawr-us, ''covered lizard'') is the animal from which this group gets its name. As you can see on page 56, the name certainly describes the animal. The most unusual feature of *Stegosaurus* is the plates that are arranged in a zigzag pattern down its back. No one is really sure what their purpose was. One guess that most scientists agree with is that the plates helped get rid of extra body heat. Just like *Dimetrodon* (pages 20–21), the amount of heat in *Stegosaurus* was controlled by the amount of blood moving through the plates and the way the animal placed its body in the wind.

Some scientists think that because the plates made the animals look bigger than they really were, enemies were scared away. Still others believe that the plates did not always stand straight up. They could perhaps be lowered to cover the sides of the body in time of danger.

It is possible that all of these guesses are right and it is just as possible that none of them is correct. Maybe you will discover the correct answer when you go digging for dinosaurs and find a *Stegosaurus* skeleton.

Ankylosaurs

Syrmosaurus

Polacanthus

Even stranger-looking than the stegosaurs were the ankylosaurs (an-KILE-o-sawrs, "curved lizards"). These dinosaurs were covered with a suit of armor. They have been called the tanks of the reptile world. They tend to stand close to the ground and look somewhat spread out.

The earliest known ankylosaur is called *Scelidosaurus* (page 37). It has been found in rocks formed during Early Jurassic time in England and Portugal.

Scelidosaurus was a slow-moving plant-eater. It was about 12 feet (a little more than three and one half meters) long and weighed about 300 pounds (about 135 kilograms). It weighed so much because it was covered with bony plates that ran from its head down to the tip of its tail. There were also small, upright plates running down the center of its back. Some scientists think that the stegosaurs and the rest of the ankylosaurs evolved from a dinosaur that was like *Scelidosaurus*. Other scientists believe that the stegosaurs and the ankylosaurs are not related.

One ankylosaur that looks a little like the stegosaurs is called *Polacanthus* (pole-a-KAN-thus, "rod edge"). It had two rows of sharp, pointed spikes along its neck and back, down to its hips. The spikes probably stuck out sideways a little instead of sticking straight up in the air. The hips were covered with spineless armor. Just below this hip cover a double row of plates ran down to the tail. *Polacanthus* lived with the last of the stegosaurs in Europe during the Early Cretaceous period.

Syrmosaurus (SEER-mo-sawr-us, "trail lizard"), from Early Cretaceous time of Mongolia, is covered entirely with armor. The armor of this 15-foot (a little over four and one half meters) ankylosaur was made of separate plates, each one with a point on it. Its head was small. It had small teeth that probably could chew only soft vegetation. The long tail was a fairly stiff rod that had a big, flat, bony enlargement at the end of it. The tail was probably swung threateningly to frighten off the large meat-eating dinosaurs that it shared the landscape with.

Stegosaurus

Stegosaurus is one of the best-known dinosaurs. It grew to be about 20 feet (over six meters) in length and was eight feet (less than two and one half meters) high at the hips. The plated backbone formed a great arch that rose about 11 feet (more than three meters) above the ground at the highest point. The front legs were shorter than the rear legs. This kept the head of *Stegosaurus* close to the ground. Judging by the shape of its teeth, *Stegosaurus* ate soft vegetation that grew on the ground.

Stegosaurus was a little bigger than the largest elephant that you see in the zoo today and probably weighed as much. It even had a feature that is found in elephants. The hind legs of *Stegosaurus* and elephants have very low knees. This is because the upper leg bone is twice as long as the lower leg bone. In both cases their legs form very straight columns to help support the large weight of their body. Their big, cushionlike feet also help distribute their weight.

Some people jokingly describe *Stegosaurus* as the animal with two brains, one in its tiny head, about the size of a walnut, and the other in the hip area, about 20 times larger. Actually, the one in the rear is not a true brain but a place where the backbone is swollen by a gathering of many nerves. These nerves probably controlled its legs and tail and coordinated movements with the brain. There was a similar, smaller nerve center in the shoulder region. The only defense from the meat-eating dinosaurs that *Stegosaurus* had was in its tail and possibly its backbone plates. The tail had two pairs of spikes that could do damage to the hide of any dinosaur.

Ankylosaurus

The ankylosaurs get their name from *Ankylosaurus* (an-KILE-o-sawr-us, "curved lizard") which is also called *Euoplocephalus* (you-o-plo-SEF-a-lus, "well-armored head"). Both names are good ones. *Ankylosaurus* could grow to be 18 feet (more than five and one half meters) long, six feet (less than two meters) wide, and weigh 6,000 pounds (about 2,730 kilograms). Like all the ankylosaurs, it was well protected from meat-eaters. Its back was covered with overlapping bony plates, as was most of its head. Even the tail was protected with these bony coverings that were shaped like rings. The tip of the tail ended in a ball of bone. Sharp spikes rimmed the sides of the bony covering on its back. Like all of the ankylosaurs, its body was broad and flattened. Its short legs gave it a squat appearance. When it was surprised by its enemies it could lie close to the ground, keeping its feet underneath its body. If a really hungry dinosaur tried to turn it over, it gave the dinosaur a bone-crunching smack with the tip of its tail. *Ankylosaurus* lived with *Tyrannosaurus* during the end of the Cretaceous period in North America.

With all the protection they had, it is surprising that the ankylosaurs became extinct.

Ankylosaurus

Extinction

Why did the dinosaurs become extinct? Why did they disappear suddenly? In this book we mention why individual kinds of dinosaurs died and how we think all the dinosaurs became extinct. We even give what seem to be good reasons for extinction.

All of the dinosaurs became extinct. But they were not alone. Many other reptiles also ceased to be—plesiosaurs, ichthyosaurs, mosasaurs, pterosaurs. Even in the groups that did not become extinct, such as the lizards, crocodiles, and turtles, there were families that vanished within these groups at the end of the Cretaceous period.

As amazing as the extinction of the reptiles seems to be, they were not the only group of animals to disappear. There were many other groups of vertebrate and invertebrate animals and plants that did so too.

What could cause the complete extinction of animals that lived in the air, in the sea, and on the land? A harder question to answer is why did some animals and plants survive. Almost all animals and plants that we find as fossils are extinct.

One attempt to explain the extinction of all these diverse groups is to look for some reason outside of the earth. The most popular guess involving extraterrestrial forces is the cosmic ray theory.

When a star explodes, all sorts of rays are released—cosmic rays, gamma rays, and X rays, among others. If the cosmic and gamma rays entered the earth's atmosphere, they would produce a tremendous amount of radiation that would be detrimental to life that is sensitive to it. Animals that live in sheltered places or deep in the ocean would be protected. Simple animals and plants are not too sensitive. But complex plants and large animals are and they would be killed.

In addition, the X rays would create mighty storms in the earth's atmosphere and cause great ice clouds to form there. The ice clouds would cause the earth to cool off because the sun's heat would be reflected away. The result—extinction of a great many plants and animals.

This is an interesting guess made to fit some facts that exist in the rock record. However, there is no astronomical evidence for it at all.

Another guess, but with many more facts to back

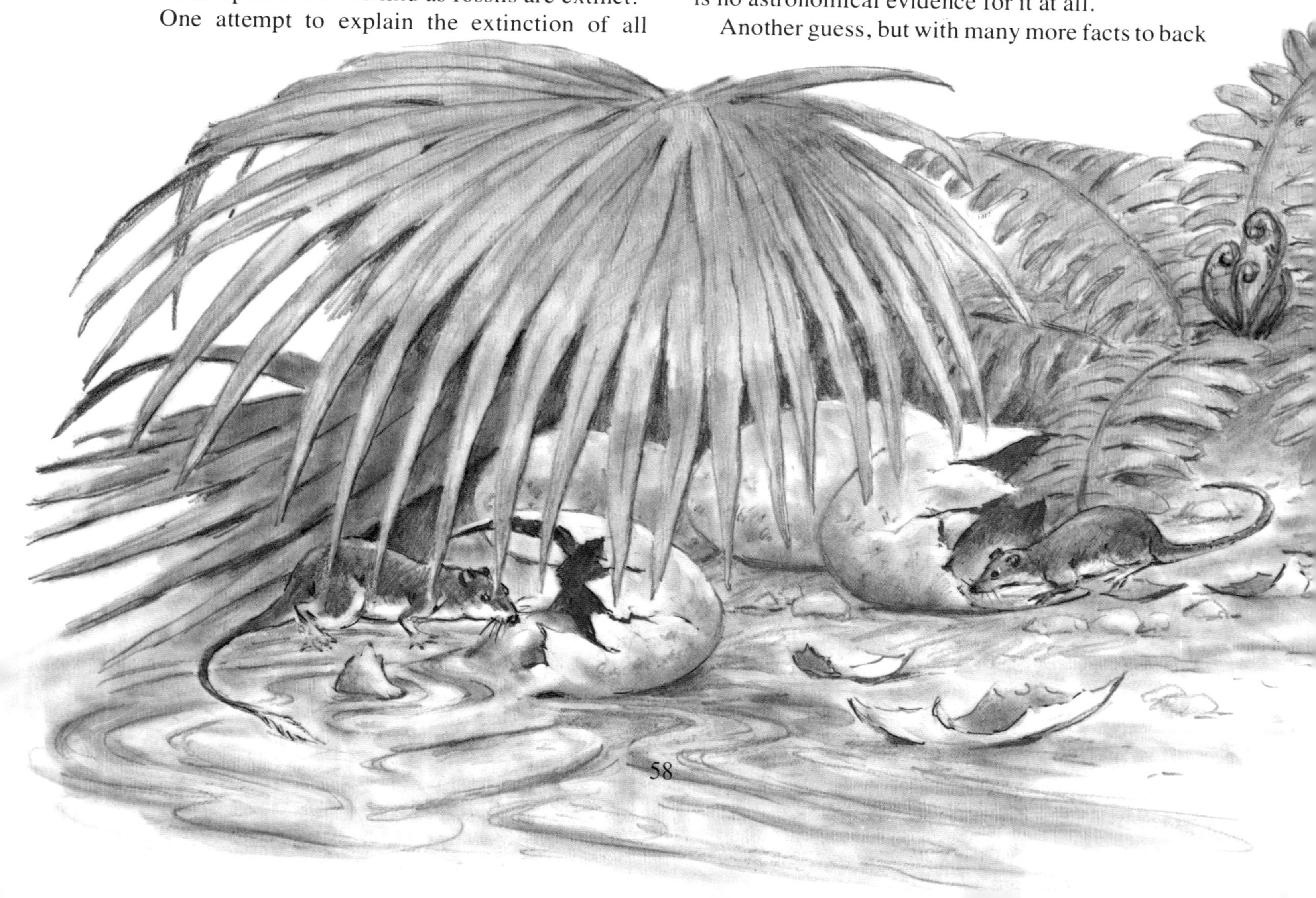

it up, concerns climatic changes on the earth. At the end of the Cretaceous period, the warm climate that existed throughout the world began to change. Warm areas shrank in size as cool ones began to expand in the polar regions. The earth began to form the climatic belts that we know today. As a result of these climatic changes, vegetation throughout the world changed. These vegetational changes first affected the plant-eating reptiles, who began to die of starvation. This in turn affected the meat-eaters, for there was no more meat for them to eat.

At the same time as the climate was changing, the land surface was changing too. Mountains such as the Rockies were being formed. These high barriers had direct effects on the climate because they changed the course of air currents that usually make the land on one side of a mountain very dry. As the land rose, the great, shallow inland seas disappeared. The continents were also changing their position in relation to one another. These two factors had a great effect on the sea animals.

Obviously, the entire food chain was affected, and a great chain reaction occurred that affected those plants and animals that could not adapt to the environmental changes. Those that adapted took over.

There are many guesses concerned directly with the extinction of the dinosaurs. One explanation suggests that the eggs of the dinosaurs were eaten by Cretaceous mammals or even the dinosaur *Ornithomimus* (see pages 38–39). Of course, if all the eggs were eaten it would eventually lead to extinction. There is no basis for this guess. A look at recent reptiles shows that they produce a great many eggs to compensate for losses due to theft or some other mishap. You can even find this in the fossil record. Eggs of *Protoceratops* have been found preserved in Mongolia in abundance.

Another theory says that the dinosaurs were destroyed by disease that spread rapidly throughout the reptile world, perhaps with the help of disease-carrying insects.

There are many more such "theories," most of them the results of a good imagination and little or no facts. The point is that there is no clear explanation for the extinction of the dinosaurs.

The Last Dinosaurs

This is the last dinosaur scene. It could be any one of a number of places in western North America—Alberta, Montana, or Wyoming—that existed at the very end of the Cretaceous period.

The climate is warm and mild temperatures extend nearly to the Arctic. We are on the western shore of a great inland sea that stretched across the middle of North America from Alaska to the Gulf of Mexico. There are many lakes and rivers flowing into the sea. The shoreline stretches back for miles, and the coastal plain is covered with dense forests.

Soon the climate will begin to change. The polar regions begin getting cooler. The reptiles begin migrating to keep within the warmer temperatures. The warm areas will be smaller than before. As a result the number of different kinds of dinosaurs will be smaller.

The land becomes more and more harsh for the dinosaurs. The warm areas no longer form a continuous belt. The dinosaurs are now living in separate regions that are no longer connected.

Even if the dinosaurs were warm-blooded, the cooler climate would have affected the eggs and young dinosaurs.

As the climate changed, so did the vegetation.

New plants took the place of older kinds that could no longer live in the cool climate. It is possible that the dinosaurs could have adapted to the new vegetation, but the environment was changing faster than the dinosaurs could adapt.

The number of individuals in separate areas continued to get smaller and smaller. They were just able to survive. Then a great mountain began to rise and the climate became even worse for the dinosaurs. The great inland sea began to dry up, as did the lakes, wide rivers, and swamps with it.

The final blow was dealt. The dinosaurs became extinct. The Age of Mammals had begun.

The mammals were small creatures who had been living side by side with the dinosaurs for millions of years. There was no real competition between them. Each had its own living quarters and food needs.

Even after the dinosaurs were gone it would take a long while for the mammals to emerge from the shrubs and tree roots and take their place in the open. Eventually some would grow to enormous size just as some dinosaurs did 150 million years ago.

INDEX